The Christian Introvert

Evan D. Baltz, M.Div.

2nd Edition Copyright © 2017 Evan D. Baltz, M.Div.
All rights reserved.
ISBN-13: 978-1540587206
ISBN-10: 1540587207

DEDICATION

This book is dedicated to all the silent Christian Introverts out there. My prayer is that you will feel this book voices your thoughts and feelings.

CONTENTS

	Acknowledgments	i
1	I Am A Christian Introvert	1
2	What Is An Introvert?	7
3	The Problem	21
4	The Bible And Introversion	29
5	Jesus Was An Introvert	35
6	The Bible And Church Ministry	51
7	How To Minister To Introverts	62
	Appendix A	67

ACKNOWLEDGMENTS

Thank you to those who have helped me understand my own introversion, which helped me to make sense of my entire life.

1
I AM A CHRISTIAN INTROVERT

I am a Christian. I am an introvert.

I have been a Christian since I accepted Christ into my life as a 5 year old. But even as a young person I never looked forward to Sunday School or church. Why? Because I wasn't a good committed Christian? No, because I am an introvert and didn't enjoy the forced social interactions. I didn't enjoy VBS. I didn't enjoy and didn't want to go to church camp. I didn't like pot luck dinners. I didn't like Bible study groups.

Why? Because I was a heretic who didn't value Bible teaching or fellowship? No. I am an introvert. I felt guilty for what I perceived was the cultural and social shaming of this personality trait for which I did not understand and recognize.

My parents, godly people who loved me dearly, did not understand and instead pressured me into uncomfortable social situations which only heightened my feelings of guilt and feeling as if I was not a good Christian because I wasn't conforming to the extroverted Christian experience.

And yet, I loved the Lord deeply and wanted to serve him. I completed Seminary. I loved the study of God's word in Seminary, but did not enjoy the social interactions which many did. I had a gift of speaking and of interpretation and communication of God's word though, and so went into ministry.

First was youth work, where most ministers start their career. I loved the one on one time with young people but was easily exhausted by the constant social youth parties and events and eventually burned out of youth ministry.

After a time in the business world, I returned to full time ministry as a senior pastor. I loved so much the weekly in-depth study of God's word and sharing it from the pulpit each Sunday. It felt like something was so right internally. And yet the social requirements of being the senior pastor in a church of about 100 people exhausted me. I soon burned out in that ministry as well, and returned to the business world where I focused on computer work that allowed me a decent amount of quiet work time. But, in that, I have felt a missing outlet for that inner desire to study and communicate God's word.

Through the years I sat in large churches and was ministered to from the pulpit. But the social nature of those large services and ministries drains me and depletes my energy rather than strengthen me. I love hearing the Word preached but don't enjoy being in the large group of people. I often feel close to a panic attack in such settings.

This continued year after year. Some Sundays I just stayed home in an effort, after an exhausting week at work, to simply recharge from alone time, but feeling guilty for not being at church.

In the 49th year of life did I finally come to understand what has been at work inside me my entire life. I am an introvert. It started with a Facebook group for introverts. Daily it encouraged me that I was normal. I was okay. I am an introvert and that is fine and anywhere from one third to one half of the population is just like me.

Sunday, October 18, 2015.

On this day, despite feeling uncomfortable in a large congregation again, I sat, near the back as usual, and listened to my pastor read from Nehemiah 2.

Early the following spring, in the month of Nisan, during the twentieth year of King Artaxerxes' reign, I was serving the king his wine. I had never before appeared sad in his presence. So the king asked me, "Why are you looking so sad? You don't look sick to me. You must be deeply troubled."

I felt this was me. I am deeply troubled. Why doesn't the church attempt to meet the introvert where they are? Why aren't there ministries specifically designed for us? There are often pastors of every social type of ministry but none that focus on ministering to introverts in a real and meaningful way.

The pastor then concluded with, "The Lord is speaking someone today…" Indeed he was. God was saying how can an introvert minister to introverts?

And that is the question that lead me to thinking about and feeling compelled to write this book.

My first goal is to help Christian introverts understand themselves and understand that God appreciates them just the way he designed them. He does not require them to become extroverts in order to be good Christians. They have much to offer the body in terms of in-depth reflective thinking and study. They can support each other in new ways.

The second goal of this book is to highlight the shortcomings of the modern church's approach, or lack of approach as the case may be, to ministering to introverts, and suggest how they might adopt new methods to better reach the millions of us out there that are Christian Introverts.

2
WHAT IS AN INTROVERT?

Fundamentally the difference between introverts and extroverts is that extroverts receive energy from being social, and introverts are drained by such interactions, Instead, introverts receive energy from being alone, quiet, contemplative.

The first time I read that definition, it was like a huge lightbulb went off in my head. THIS IS ME! It rang so true that it virtually brought me to tears. Why hadn't I read or understood this earlier in life. It could have made such a difference. I had taken the Myers-Briggs personality exam several times for business, but had never really contemplated the introversion scale (I'm 92% introverted) much in the past. I didn't really see myself as an introvert. I'm not sure why I didn't see the signs, but they were all there. It was like I was living in denial. Probably because I had bought into the popular myths of what it meant to be an introvert.

Carl King has succinctly debunked 10 popular introvert myths that helped me come to grips with my own identity.

Myth #1: Introverts don't like to talk.

This is not true. Introverts just don't talk unless they have something to say. They hate small talk. Get an introvert talking about something they are interested in, and they won't shut up for days.

Those who know me best, are often surprised when I say I am introverted. They don't usually see it. When I am with them, because I am comfortable with them, I chat up a storm. I can even be the life of the party, if the group is small and consists of people I trust. When you get me talking about certain topics, I won't shut up. But indeed I do hate small talk. I'm terrible with just the day to day chit chat with acquaintances, other soccer parents, friends of friends, waiters, people in elevators etc…Because of this, some people perceive me like #2, #3 or #4 that follow.

Knowing that other people might also be like this, I tend to gravitate toward the least talkative people in a desire to discover what that topic is for them. It's so fun to see and introvert open up when you find it. What are those topics for you? How do you feel about small talk? Have others ever misperceived you?

Myth #2: Introverts are shy.

> *Shyness has nothing to do with being an Introvert. Introverts are not necessarily afraid of people. What they need is a reason to interact. They don't interact for the sake of interacting. If you want to talk to an Introvert, just start talking. Don't worry about being polite.*

This is probably the most common misperception. If you are like me, you might not be afraid of people, but rather anxious about unplanned interactions. Because of that, introverts often won't start conversations, especially with people they don't know.

Myth #3: Introverts are rude.

> *Introverts often don't see a reason for beating around the bush with social pleasantries. They want*

> *everyone to just be real and honest. Unfortunately, this is not acceptable in most settings, so Introverts can feel a lot of pressure to fit in, which they find exhausting.*

How many times has a parent or teacher suggested that you were being rude? They don't understand that you just want to cut to the chase or dispense with the pleasantries. There is nothing wrong with not being ebullient. The pressures to be like extroverts can often drive introverts even deeper into isolation. The more pressure, the more we pull away.

Myth #4: Introverts don't like people.

> *On the contrary, Introverts intensely value the few friends they have. They can count their close friends on one hand. If you are lucky enough for an introvert to consider*

you a friend, you probably have a loyal ally for life. Once you have earned their respect as being a person of substance, you're in.

This can also be a double-edged sword, because if one of those friends in the inner circle betrays us or just walks away from the friendship, it hurts the introvert deeply. That person represents a large percentage of their trust circle. It can cause an introvert to question other friendships and circle the wagons even tighter. Introverts need their friends. They don't have a high turnover rate in this group. Introverts tend to find places and situations where they can have long-time relationships, so they are less likely to want to move.

Moving a lot as a young person can seriously effect introverted children. They have very carefully selected a close group of friends. But then mom and dad decide to move. This upsets their entire world. They will have to start all over again in a new city, and this is a daunting task and can often lead young introverts to give up making new friends for a time because it is so draining. Parents of young introverts should carefully consider their children's well-being before moving and upsetting their child's social environment. Please don't dismissively say, "Oh you'll make new friends." That is perceived by your son or daughter as, "We don't care at all about you."

With Facebook and email and other social media options today, the sting of moving is reduced slightly, but it is still unbelievably scary and upsetting to an introvert child.

My family moved many times and the move between my 6th grade and 7th grade years was particular difficult. I wrote a very heart-felt note to my father and put it in his medicine cabinet for him to see in the morning. In it I pleaded with him not to move us. I told him if he really loved me, he wouldn't make me move. For a 12 year old to express that, you can tell how major of an event this was for me. I didn't know all the depth of the reasons for those emotions at the time, but I understand them now.

> ***Myth #5: Introverts don't like to go out in public.***
>
> *Nonsense. Introverts just don't like to go out in public FOR AS LONG. They also like to avoid the complications that are involved in public activities. They take in data and experiences very quickly, and as a result, don't need to be there for long to "get it." They're ready to go home, recharge, and process it all. In fact, recharging is absolutely crucial for Introverts.*

You might plan your social activities down to the minute. I review maps of how to get to the place I'm going, so I don't get lost or need to ask directions. I check on parking availability. I make sure to have "an out" if I don't like the location or people or activity. I usually only go if a close trusted friend is going as well. I don't like the hassle. This is a big reason that introverts often like to work from home when possible. We would also generally prefer to go out in nature than be in a big group social environment. This fact is going to play heavily into my indictment of the modern church.

Myth #6: Introverts always want to be alone.

Introverts are perfectly comfortable with their own thoughts. They think a lot. They daydream. They like to have problems to work on, puzzles to solve. But they can also get incredibly lonely if they don't have anyone to share their discoveries with. They crave an authentic and sincere connection with ONE PERSON at a time.

We don't always want to be alone, but we need more alone time. We love one on one interactions and prefer them to group settings.

Has this ever happened to you? You plan to meet a friend for coffee or dinner and you are looking forward to this one on one time with your friend. When you arrive, your friend has brought along another friend or two with them. I can hear the "You just lost" game show music playing. Of course we adapt and get through it but are disappointed with the bait and switch we hadn't planned for mentally.

For parents, plan more one on one time play dates for your children instead of throwing them into parties and groups. And be sure to share quality one on one time with them yourself.

Myth #7: Introverts are weird.

Introverts are often individualists. They don't follow the crowd. They'd prefer to be valued for their novel ways of living. They think for themselves and because of that, they often challenge the norm. They don't make most decisions based on what is popular or trendy.

Some of the most influential people in history have been introverts, so don't worry, you are in good "weird" company. People like, Albert Einstein, Bill Gates, Abraham Lincoln, and Elon Musk, were/are introverts.

Myth #8: Introverts are aloof nerds.

Introverts are people who primarily look inward, paying close attention to their thoughts and emotions. It's not that they are incapable of paying attention to what is going on around them, it's just that their inner world is much more stimulating and rewarding to them.

Many of us would be rich if we had a nickel for every time someone called us aloof. What they perceive as aloofness is nothing more than us approaching social situations differently than them. Do you think they would be surprised that we think they are "loud" and "obnoxious"?

Myth #9: Introverts don't know how to relax and have fun.

Introverts typically relax at home or in nature, not in busy public places. Introverts are not thrill seekers and adrenaline junkies. If there is too much talking and noise going on, they shut down. Their brains are too sensitive to the neurotransmitter called Dopamine. Introverts and Extroverts have

different dominant neuro-pathways.
Just look it up.

I love silence. I want to control the amount of stimulus coming in. So if the baseline is silent, then I can control how many distractions are added to that. In crowded and noisy situations, introverts tend to just observe and find ways to minimize the stimulus. Doing something "boring" is often our greatest desire. We don't consider confusion and crowds as "fun".

Myth #10: Introverts can fix themselves and become Extroverts.

A world without Introverts would be a world with few scientists, musicians, artists, poets, filmmakers, doctors, mathematicians, writers, and philosophers. That being said, there are still plenty of techniques an Extrovert can learn in order to

> *interact with Introverts. Introverts cannot "fix themselves" and deserve respect for their natural temperament and contributions to the human race. In fact, one study (Silverman, 1986) showed that the percentage of Introverts increases with IQ.*

Most introverts feel betrayed when others, or books, or teachers, or parents tell us we just need to change and become more like them or more like extroverts. We don't want to be someone else. We want to be ourselves. We want you to understand us and accept us for who we are. We don't want to be forced into accepting your worldview. And, we hate being made to feel guilty because we don't like the same things you like. This leads us to a key problem within the modern church's approach to ministry.

3
THE PROBLEM

The modern Christian church, perhaps especially the evangelical church, is designed almost exclusively for extroverted individuals.

What's wrong with this model? It excludes or even alienates and fails to minister effectively to perhaps as much as 50% of the population.

Using Myers-Briggs evaluations, 50.9% of those surveyed fall into one of the 8 introverted personality types. Other recent surveys have also backed up this data, so it is fairly safe to say fully ½ the population is or leans toward introversion.

This also means that it's likely 50% of the people sitting in the pew each week at church are introverted and therefore likely uncomfortable in that environment.

So why does the modern church continue to focus on that model? Do you believe that this assertion is accurate? How about some examples:

1. Sunday Worship Service – This traditional and most common form of church ministry almost exclusively involves a large meeting of hundreds or thousands of people in a sanctuary or auditorium. It also generally involves singing out loud in public surrounded by strangers. Many churches expect church goers to stand and greet and shake hands with strangers. Interestingly enough, nowhere in scripture is there any mention of, or requirement for, such a "service" and it was completely unknown to the first century Christian. Instead they met in small groups in homes. Instead of following the early church examples, mega-churches have continued to blossom and take over most smaller congregations. Megachurches spend millions and millions of dollars on facilities, building bigger and bigger buildings and campuses which require higher and higher maintenance budgets. Their Sunday services are more like concerts which involve video screens, high tech audio systems, and large capacity auditoriums.

2. Sunday School Classes – Generally a smaller group than a full worship service, but often still a large group of people in a room where interaction is often an encouraged method of "study". A recent Sunday School class I attended at a large evangelical church consisted of nearly 500 people.

3. Small Groups – Many churches have "small" groups which consist of meeting in another's home with 10-15 other individuals with whom you may or may not know personally. These groups encourage social interaction as a major component. This is closer to the biblical model, but is only part of the church's programs. To an introvert, a small group would probably be about 4-6 people at most. Often these small groups consist of 15-20 minutes of chit-chat, a few minutes of study, followed up with additional social chit-chat over coffee and snacks.

4. Bible Studies – Bible studies are generally a gathering of people that vary in size but generally involve a social component. Church wide Bible studies may even involve hundreds of men or women in a large meeting environment. My current church has both men and women large-scale Bible studies that meet in the church auditorium and consist of hundreds of members.

5. Social Events – Most churches have regular social events such as pot luck dinners, picnics, or other large-scale gatherings of people where social interaction is the primary focus. Take a look at your church's calendar. It likely consists of many of these events. A quick glance at my own church calendar shows a Color Run (hundreds of people), a men's breakfast (probably 50 or so men), and a newcomers luncheon.

6. Ministry Opportunities – Most ministry opportunities involve teaching a group of individuals (often children or young people), witnessing to strangers, ushering during a worship service, or singing or taking part in a choir. Almost all of these are completely out of the question for most introverts. One might even ask if introverts CAN even minister to others based on these options. We'll address that later on.

7. Church Camp – For young people and adults, yearly church camps or "retreats" involve large groups of people "getting away" to socialize with others. My own experience with church camps still gives me chills, and not in a good way.

The first time I went to church camp was when I was in 4th grade. I went to a very large Christian camp in the woods of Minnesota. There were nearly 500 other 4th through 6th grade boys there. And I thought a school classroom of 25 was bad. Myself and several other friends from my church were in a cabin with 6-8 other total strangers. Having not been to junior high yet, most of us had never even changed our clothes around anyone other than our family, and yet here we were with complete strangers and expected to do so. Needless to say, I did not take a shower the entire week. Everything we did for an entire agonizing week was with a group. We ate in a group, we sat in services in a group, we swam as a group and slept as a group. It really was about my worst nightmare. I didn't know why I hated it so much at the time, but now, knowing that I was an introvert, it all makes sense. Some of my other friends loved it. I couldn't understand why? They couldn't understand why I didn't like it. That is almost always the case with introverts and extroverts.

On the one occasion I attempted to get some alone time I was scolded by a camp leader, and told to go back to the group. And, of course there were this many young boys, you can imagine the amount of noise and commotion. It was never ending. It really was a traumatic experience and it took me weeks to recover from it when I got home. Of course no one understood.

Two years later as a 6th grader I was forced to go back to the camp again. No one could understand why I didn't want to go. I could not articulate it. I just didn't want to go. I didn't understand why, I just knew that I did not want to. Second verse, same as the first. That was the last time I ever went to camp (save several family camp experiences which were not any better).

There are certainly more examples of these types of church ministries, but I think anyone can recognize and see the pattern.

This is how the modern church has functioned for as long as anyone can remember, so why is this a problem?

These are all extrovert focused activities, and, as we mentioned, according to recent research, as much as 50% of the population are introverts. So is the modern churching ministering effectively to only half of its congregation? If so, this is perhaps one of the biggest oversights of the modern church. Churches have become bigger and bigger. Churches proudly boast of ministering to sometimes tens of thousands of people through their huge mega-auditorium so-called "seeker sensitive" socially popular performance-based services. And yet it is this exact type of activity which is the last type of activity most introverts would desire to involve themselves in on a regular basis.

Worse than that, introverts are often made to feel as if they aren't being "good Christians" when they buck this extroverted trend. We are guilt-tripped by Joe Gladhander and Jane Gadfly. We are told we need to be more like them, the extroverts, if we want to please God and minister in the church. Making someone feel guilty for just being who they are is especially painful and discouraging. I believe many introverted Christians have left churches because of this.

4
THE BIBLE AND INTROVERSION

Does the Bible have anything to say about introversion? To begin with, the Scriptures often speak of quiet introspection as critical to closeness to God.

"Be still, and know that I am God!" Psalm 46:10

The Hebrew for the command to "be still" is a rare word from a root that means to cease, abandon, alone, fall limp. The Psalmist is describing God's desire for his people to just stop being busy, because it is that constant motion and striving and busyness that cause his people to lose focus of who God is and what God does. Being still is often one of an introvert's favorite states of being. When we sit quietly and stare, our mind has time to adjust to the stillness and begin to focus on God. It strengthens the introvert physically, mentally, emotionally, and spiritually.

I would guess that for most extroverts, being still causes them to be anxious and feel disconnected.

"...but Jacob had a quiet temperament, preferring to stay at home."
Genesis 25:27

Isaac's two sons were quite different. The older, Esau was his father's favorite and probably the most natural of the two to be a leader and find favor with God. But, as Paul reminds us in Romans 9:13, "Just as it is written: "Jacob I loved, but Esau I hated." God's favor was on Jacob, the man of quiet temperament. So God can certainly work through and with introverts.

There is nothing wrong with you if you have a quiet temperament and prefer to stay at home. You are just like Jacob. And who was Jacob? Genesis 35:10 says, "God said to him, "Your name is Jacob, but you will no longer be called Jacob; your name will be Israel." So he named him Israel." So this introverted man became the name of God's chosen nation!

"But when you pray, go away by yourself, shut the door behind you, and pray to your Father in private. Then your Father, who sees everything, will reward you."
Matthew 6:6

Why would Jesus instruct his followers to pray in this manner? In contrast to the Pharisees and "religious" of the day, who stood in public in synagogues or street corners and recited their selfish prayers, Jesus knew that true communion with God (the very definition of prayer) should most often happen in silence. Being alone with God helps the believer commune with Him and remove the distractions of the world. This is great for introverts as being alone in a private, quiet place, is perfectly in keeping with our natural tendencies. Prayer in this environment for us renews our strength. Being in public, such as a church service or with a Bible study group is often draining and feels awkward for the introvert. Jesus certainly isn't saying that we should never pray in public, but real communication with God is most likely to take place in the quiet environment.

Asking an introvert to pray in public may be met with great apprehension. Not because they aren't confident in their relationship with God, but rather they prefer to follow the instructions of Jesus from Matthew 6:6. Please respect Christian introverts in this behavior and desire.

> *"Make it your goal to live a quiet life, minding your own business and working with your hands, just as we instructed you before. Then people who are not believers will respect the way you live, and you will not need to depend on others."*
>
> 1 Thessalonians 4:11-12

Paul is telling Christians in the church the best way to live their lives. It sounds like he is suggesting something more in line with an introverted lifestyle. But at least, for introverts, this should be a great encouragement that Paul believes living your life in a quiet way is good. In fact, he suggests it's actually a way, perhaps the best way, to witness to others. Imagine that! You don't hear a lot sermons preached like that. You don't see a lot of discipleship and evangelism classes teaching living a quiet life. Why not? Is it because church leaders are often extroverted and believe that evangelism can only be done through extroverted means? This doesn't seem to be the model that the Apostle Paul is suggesting.

All of these Scriptures should encourage the introverted Christian. Who you are is respected and promoted in God's Word. In fact, there is even a bigger encouragement for us that I see in Scripture.

5
JESUS WAS AN INTROVERT

Jesus was an introvert. There I said it.

Think about it. Your first thoughts are probably it can't be so. Wasn't Jesus always around people? Didn't Jesus speak to large groups? Didn't Jesus travel around meeting new people all the time? How could he have been an introvert?

Previously though, we looked at myths about introversion. We learned that introverts may often be able to, or called to, do things that aren't necessarily in their comfort zone or preferred state. I'm an introvert, but used to be a youth pastor and senior pastor. I spoke to large groups of people. The indicator though was that these activities drained me of strength. I would rather be by myself writing and studying than in a large group. Sometimes your job calls you to do these tasks and you do them. It doesn't mean that it is your preferred state and likely these tasks drain you.

Think back to the last time at work you had to lead a meeting or speak to a group. How did you feel after? Or how about that last work party? You might have even enjoyed it for a time, but after you were completely exhausted.

So we can't always determine who is an introvert or an extrovert based on outward signs. As I noted earlier, many of my friends can't believe I am introverted. They don't see that side of me. They don't know how exhausted I am after having been with them.

Let's look at Jesus' life. He went into the family business, probably at a young age. He was a carpenter. Mark 6:3 tells us, *"Isn't this the carpenter? Isn't this Mary's son and the brother of James, Joseph, Judas and Simon? Aren't his sisters here with us? And they took offense at him."*

The Greek word translated "carpenter" is tektón *(τέκτων)* which means a craftsman, artisan, specifically a carpenter. In a recent article by Laurie Pawlik-Kienlen, she lists some of the best jobs for quiet introverted people:

- Truck driver
- Artist
- Photographer
- On air personality (radio DJ)
- Internet technology or computer programming
- Night cleaning person/janitor
- Night watchman
- Lab worker or researcher
- Trades: ***carpenters***, plumbers, landscapers
- Science: geologist, pathologist, engineer, statistician, actuary
- Finance: accountant, stock broker, bookkeeper

Now in the first century, very few of those vocations would have been available. But certainly one stands out, doesn't it? (My bold and italics probably helped as well.)

Carpentry was, and still is, a great job for an introvert. It provides a great deal of alone time, time to be creative, and time to work with your hands. For the first 30 years of his life, Jesus was able to enjoy this quiet lifestyle. The Bible tells us nothing about his life from age 12 until 30, except to tell us that he was a carpenter from Nazareth. He was unexceptional and of little note. In fact, those in town were offended by him, probably because they thought, "Who is this nobody carpenter? He's no teacher!"

Jesus lived this quiet life for 18 years prior to the beginning of his ministry. We can probably assume he was content in this vocation, befitting his disposition.

At 30 years of age, Jesus began his public ministry. This was his calling on earth: to teach the world about himself and about the Father, and the way of salvation. Even though this was a public ministry, Jesus still exhibited traits of his introverted nature. It should be remembered that Jesus was 100%

God, AND 100% man. This combination of his nature is known as the hypostatic union. It's a big name for the personal union of the two natures of Jesus. In His humanness, Jesus was introverted. In his Godness, Jesus was perfect. Which means he was perfectly suited to do the work and ministry that God had sent him to earth to do. He completed it perfectly. His human nature did not need to change to complete the task. Your nature does not need to change in order for you to complete the tasks God has set for you. This is a wonderfully freeing thought. I can be me and do God's work. You can be you and do God's work!

Let's look at some examples that point to Jesus' introversion during his public ministry.

"Early the next morning Jesus went out to an isolated place. The crowds searched everywhere for him"

Luke 4:42

Luke tells us that Jesus was trying to get away from the crowds for some moments of solitude and peace and quiet. With all the public speaking and healing and being constantly surrounded by people, Jesus desired time alone.

My father was a pastor. He was an early riser. And by early, I mean EARLY. He would often get up at 4:30 or 5:00am. He loved to get a cup of coffee and enjoy the relative stillness of that time of day. It was dark, it was quiet. There was no commotion. No phones ringing. I asked him on several occasions why he would want to get up so early in the morning. "I just like to," he would usually say. I think he was a closet introvert. He was often silent for hours on long family car rides. He would be exhausted after Sunday morning church and take long naps on Sunday afternoon. He disliked people just showing up at the door or calling the house unexpectedly.

I never thought I would ever be a morning person like that. But when a job required it for a time, I quickly saw what my dad enjoyed about that time of the morning. It was so peaceful. There was time to gather your thoughts before the day. There was silence that allowed you to think and process. To this day, whether I actually get up early or not, I still need at least a half an hour of quiet time in the morning. It's essential in preparing for the day.

Jesus was likely doing the same in the instance that Luke is telling us about. In fact later on in Luke 5:3, Luke records that Jesus asked Simon (Peter) to take him out on to the lake so he could put some distance between himself and the crush of the crowds. Jesus was looking for some personal space.

> *Yet the news about him spread all the more, so that crowds of people came to hear him and to be healed of their sicknesses. But Jesus often withdrew to lonely places and prayed.*
> *Luke 5:15-16*

Jesus often told others to keep things on the down low (see verse 14 of Luke 5). He was seeking to not draw unnecessary attention to himself. When the crowds came, he often withdrew. He wanted to be alone, in peace, to meditate and pray. Are you starting to see the pattern? Are you starting to see how Jesus was in fact an introvert?

One Sabbath Jesus was going through the grainfields...
Luke 6:1

Why would Jesus be walking through a grainfield? Think about it this way, why would YOU walk through a grainfield? I live in a desert, so there are not many grainfields, but I love to walk through the desert. Why? Because it is quiet. Because it is beautiful. Because it allows me to be alone and think. How about you? Do you walk through "grainfields"?

One of those days Jesus went out to a mountainside to pray, and spent the night praying to God.

Luke 6:12

Again Luke tells us that Jesus got away. Perhaps because Luke was a physician he was more sensitive to Jesus' mental and physical state, and therefore records many of these moments. Perhaps Luke was an introvert himself, and so recognized this character in Jesus and chose to identify with it. This time Jesus found a mountainside. Mountainsides are favorite spots for introverts. There is something so peaceful about sitting on a mountain and overlooking an open area. It helps to free up our minds and gives us a sense of internal peace. Jesus enjoyed this spot so much that he spent the whole night there in prayer. What a wonderful picture this paints. Jesus, by himself, perhaps on his knees or sitting on a rock, staring out over the land, in quiet prayer to his Father. Perhaps he was looking toward the heavens and watching the stars. It's a very serene picture. I bought my house because it has a view of a mountain. I spend countless hours just sitting and staring at the mountain. There is something so peaceful about it. It's God's nature. It's quiet. It's majestic. It is never boring and never gets old. Do you have a special place like this? I'm willing to bet most introverts do.

One day Jesus said to his disciples, "Let us go over to the other side of the lake." So they got into a boat and set out. As they sailed, he fell asleep.
Luke 8:22

Again, why would Jesus ask his disciples to take him to the other side of the lake? In the verses leading up to this one, large crowds had been gathering around him and following him. Jesus wanted to get in a boat and find a quiet spot on the other side of the lake. Exhausted from the crowds, Jesus even fell asleep on the boat. Not long after, a storm arose and the disciples awoke him. Jesus rebuked the wind and waves and the storm subsided. Have you ever wanted to rebuke noise and commotion and make it go away?

Would that be an amazing power! One gets the feeling from this episode that Jesus was perhaps a little upset about being disturbed from his sleep and so rebuked the storm and chastised his disciples for their lack of faith. I see it as a beautiful moment of convergence of his hypostatic union.

Then he took them with him and they withdrew by themselves to a town called Bethsaida, but the crowds learned about it and followed him.
Luke 9:10-11

Jesus tries to get away with disciples to a quiet location away from the crowds. But the word always spread, and the crowds would find him. He was welcoming when they did. He patiently taught them and healed them. But when he had an opportunity to get away he did.

> *Once when Jesus was praying in private and his disciples were with him, he asked them, "Who do the crowds say I am?"*
> *Luke 9:18*

I think Jesus was attempting to teach his disciples about getting away in private to pray. He had taught this was the way to pray, and he was demonstrating it to them constantly. Being in a quiet, private place was the perfect place for Jesus to renew his spirit and commune with God. And, it was likely his preferred state. Have you noticed too, that Jesus is not instructing his disciples to go gather up a crowd of people so that he can preach to them? He hasn't rented a building or set up a tent. It's all organic.

> *About eight days after Jesus said this, he took Peter, John and James with him and went up onto a*

mountain to pray.

Luke 9:28

Jesus had circles of friends. The widest circle were the following crowds. They were likely there just for the healing and teaching. The second ring included the disciples and their friends and families and some of Jesus' other friends. The next ring was the 12 disciples. And, inside that group were his closest friends, Peter, John, and James. Even inside that was John, the disciple whom Jesus loved, i.e. Jesus' closest and most trusted friend.

What do your circles look like? Most introverts have very few really close and trusted friends, just like Jesus. We'd prefer to spend time one on one with them or in just a very small group. It looks as if Jesus had this same personal relationship structure.

Each day Jesus was teaching at the temple, and each evening he went out to spend the night on the

hill called the Mount of Olives.
Luke 21:37

While in Jerusalem, Jesus was teaching all day long. Likely exhausted from this, he would retreat to the hills. It was his place of solace. It was a place for him to renew his strength and prepare for the next day.

He withdrew about a stone's throw beyond them, knelt down and prayed.
Luke 22:41

Jesus went back to his favorite spot at the Mount of Olives with his disciples, but even withdrew further from them to pray. He knew what was about to happen and needed to pray alone. So distraught was he, that an angel from heaven came and strengthened him. Jesus would not have another minute to himself for days.

> *Early in the morning, Jesus stood on the shore, but the disciples did not realize that it was Jesus.*
>
> John 21:4

After the resurrection, Jesus made numerous appearances. This special one mentioned in John, notes again that Jesus was up early in the morning. Even in his resurrected state, Jesus is still seen as being up early in the morning and by the sea shore. One last quiet peaceful moment on earth. Another beautiful picture. Think of Jesus, his amazing work and ministry completed. Now before he ascends to heaven until he comes again, he is standing in the sand on the shore of a lake. Probably very calm and peaceful. Jesus was taking it all in. This would be his last moments on earth and last interactions with his disciples. It's a wonderful moment. And what do people usually do when they stand on the shore of a lake? Often I pick up stones and skip them. Maybe you dip your toes in the water to test the temperature.

Maybe you close your eyes and listen to the waves. I can picture Jesus doing all of these things.

So I began this chapter with the declarative statement that Jesus was an introvert. Are you convinced? Read through the Gospels again to yourself, but this time through, note all these occasions. You may find others as well that point to Jesus' human nature and his introversion. As a Christian introvert, knowing that my Lord and Savior understands my inner being, and relates to who I am, it encourages me and strengthens me. It helps me to know that I can be myself. How does it make you feel?

How does Christ's church on earth now minister to those of us who are introverts?

6
THE BIBLE AND CHURCH MINISTRY

Is the church telling Christians to be "good" Christians, socially acceptable Christians, they must be extroverted Christians? From the summary of common church ministries, it would appear so. Thus ignoring ½ of its congregation's spiritual and personal needs.

Perhaps there is a mandate in Scripture, either by Jesus or from the Apostles, that stipulates the church should function in such a way as to cater to extroverts. Perhaps the modern evangelical church is just following instructions found in Scripture.

Let's examine some passages about the church and see if that is the case.

Therefore go and make disciples of all nations, baptizing them in the name of the Father and of the Son and of the Holy Spirit, and teaching them to obey everything I have commanded you. And surely I am with you always, to the very end of the age."
Matthew 28:19-20

This is the Great Commission. These are Jesus' final instructions to his disciples on what their calling is after Jesus' return to heaven. The main thrust of this commission it to make disciples around the world through baptism and teaching obedience to scripture/Jesus' teachings. So in terms of methods for accomplishing this mission, teaching is really the only piece that can be seen as a method.

What do we know about the effectiveness of teaching? Most schools and universities advertise their student to teacher ratio, where fewer students per teacher equals better. Why is that? Most research suggests that individualized attention and student accountability are among the key benefits. It would seem a natural step to then to apply this philosophy to teaching within the church. This might suggest smaller church groups, rather than larger, where teachers and pastors can give more individual attention and create better accountability, both very important to making disciples.

When they arrived, they went upstairs to the room where they were staying. Those present were Peter, John, James and Andrew; Philip and Thomas, Bartholomew and Matthew; James son of Alphaeus and Simon the Zealot, and

> *Judas son of James. They all joined together constantly in prayer, along with the women and Mary the mother of Jesus, and with his brothers.*
>
> *Acts 1:13-14*

These are the very first meetings of "the church". A small group meeting to pray. Before long this group grew to about 120 (Acts 1:15) with Peter as the key leader. Peter's bold preaching bore fruit with at least 3000 others joining the church in Jerusalem as believers. With this size of group, what did the church do next?

> *They devoted themselves to the apostles' teaching and to fellowship, to the breaking of bread and to prayer. Everyone was filled with awe at the many wonders and signs performed by the apostles. All the believers were together and had everything in*

> *common. They sold property and possessions to give to anyone who had need. Every day they continued to meet together in the temple courts. They broke bread in their homes and ate together with glad and sincere hearts, praising God and enjoying the favor of all the people. And the Lord added to their number daily those who were being saved.*
>
> *Acts 2:42-47*

This passage is often used to support the meeting together of the church. And, in fact, it does support that. However, let's look a little more closely at precisely what is being described in these verses.

Two key elements are mentioned first: teaching and fellowship. Teaching is always the primary focus as it was the key message of the Great Commission we looked at earlier. Added to that now is the concept of fellowship (gk. koinonia – κοινωνία). This is the sharing of and participation in something together. In connotes intimacy and closeness. One might question whether or not true koinonia can exist in very large groups, say of a hundreds or thousands because the dynamic of the group in that size often changes from one of participation and intimacy to one of a more passive observer or audience member. The examples of this fellowship listed here in Acts are meeting in the Temple courts, most likely in prayer at the normal temple prayer times, and breaking bread in their own homes. Partaking in communion in the privacy of their own homes would suggest either just family groups or smaller extended groups that could be accommodated in a single home. This closeness and intimacy helped bind the believers together in strong sub-groups. In either case, there is not the idea of this group building or buying large meeting places, but rather praying together at the temple and meeting in homes.

Clearly God desires that Christians would meet together and encourage one another. There is no question about that. This koinonia is essential for individual growth and discipleship. However, there also isn't really any suggestion or prescription for what we might see as the modern church, meeting in a large building, less frequently, and with larger groups of people. I'm not suggesting this is antithetical to the church per se, rather that Scripture certainly does not prescribe this modern method in any way. The focus appears to be on smaller, more private groups meeting in homes.

Finally, the passage tells us that it was the Lord who added to their numbers every day. The purpose of the church is to equip and disciple and teach. It is God, through the Holy Spirit, that brings individuals to a saving faith.

I am writing to Philemon, our beloved co-worker, and to our sister Apphia, and to our fellow soldier Archippus, and to the church that meets in your house.
Philemon 1:1-2

A church met in the house of Archippus (possibly Philemon's son). This is another example of how the early church met. They met in houses. Small groups. But wasn't the church here in Colossae much larger than just a house church? Yes. We must look at how the word "church" is used. The church universal is all believers. The church in a city or region, like Colossae or Ephesus, is a reference to all believers in that city or region. In each of those areas there would be many small groups that met in houses. This is the local church – a small group of believers. No doubt on occasion the various local churches would meet together or share resources, but their daily/weekly meetings for prayer and fasting and fellowship were in homes.

It might be argued that as these home churches grew in size it became a natural progression to secure a larger meeting place. And as additional resources became available, the group could build a designated building for that meeting and the whole thing snowballed into the mega-churches of today which have campuses which can accommodate tens of thousands of church goers.

But is that the natural progression? Why couldn't the church continue to grow, as it did in Jerusalem and Colossae and Ephesus and other cities, by more people hosting church groups in their homes? Why is that not a more preferable progression? Think of the benefits of the home church:

- No or little overhead. Church buildings require ever increasing resources and financial support, whereas a home meeting requires almost nothing. Money can be spent and shared directly with those in need.
- Small groups mean individualized teaching.
- Small church groups grow through natural relationships. Members know and care about those with whom they fellowship.
- Intimate fellowship, the meaning of the word koinonia, leading to detailed and personal prayer requests.
- The ability to easily meet regularly/daily.
- Accountability.

Thinking back to how many introverts there might be in the general population, this model for a church would also be much more agreeable to those of us of that disposition.

> *Make it your goal to live a quiet life,
> minding your own business and working
> with your hands, just as we instructed you
> before. Then people who are not Christians
> will respect the way you live, and you will
> not need to depend on others.*
> *1 Thessalonians 4:11-12*

Here is Paul's succinct instructions to the members of the church in Thessalonica. Live a quiet life. Work with your hands (like say a carpenter would?). Doing so will cause others to respect you.

I love this instruction so much. To me, it's Paul telling introverts their way of life and who they are as people is perfectly in tune with God's desire for their lives. In fact it's the preferred way for Christians to live and act. The next time another Christian in the church tells you that you should be more extroverted and outwardly social, simply explain this verse to them. You are just being obedient to Paul's teaching.

How does this make you feel? Does it give you a new sense of peace and contentment with who you are? Does the Biblical insight into the early church seem to present a local church that would be more appealing to you? How should the local church seek to minister to introverts?

7
HOW TO MINISTER TO INTROVERTS

Why doesn't the church attempt to meet the introvert where they are? Why aren't there ministries specifically designed for us? There are often pastors of every social type of ministry but none that focus on ministering to introverts in a real and meaningful way.

Having been in ministry, I know first-hand that it is easy to complain about things within the church. It is important however to always offer and discuss suggestions and solutions. So here are some suggestions. It may be up to you to share these with your church (perhaps give them a copy of this book) because it is unlikely traditional churches and ministers will even know about these issues or be looking to solve them.

1:1 Bible Studies – Most churches offer larger group Bible studies, but what would be even more meaningful for introverts would be a one-on-one study. Just two people meeting to study God's word. Perhaps a directed study from a book, or just reading a passage and discussing.

Internet/Forum Bible Study Groups – Study passages (perhaps the same ones as the larger groups) but do so independently and then discuss in either a live chat or a forum type internet setting.

Biblical Question and Answer Site – Anyone can ask any question and it is researched and studied and answered responsibly by the minister to introverts.

Weekly Online Bible Study Questions for Individual Study – A series of questions for the study of a given passage of Scripture. Individuals would research and study the passage on their own and respond. They could then interact with others about the answers. *(See appendix A)*

Video messages with real-time internet chat following – The technology exists now to make this easy. Facebook allows live streaming and a church could easily live stream their morning service. Viewers could watch and interact from home. This way they could enjoy the same message and music, but avoid some of the social anxiety of the large church service.

Resource support for introverts in their everyday lives – This could be in the form a pastor specifically designated to minister to introverts. He could meet them for coffee or lunch, challenge them through emails, and interact with them online in other ways.

1:1 prayer support teams – Individuals could meet for one-on-one prayer or communicate through email/chat, sharing prayer concerns and answers.

I challenge all churches to consider these alternate forms of ministry. I also challenge churches to re-examine the Biblical model for the early church. It is quite possible that as much as 50% of your congregation are introverts. They come to church each week with a certain amount of apprehension. Please show us you care. Please acknowledge that we exist and accept us as we are and minister to us in ways that are more meaningful to us. Any time you create a new event or ministry, please consider us. Don't leave us out. Don't leave us behind. We love God. We want to study His word. We are Christians, and we are introverts.

APPENDIX A
1 Thessalonians Q&A Bible Study

This is a sample of what a weekly question and answer Bible study might look like. These questions could be posted weekly to a church website or emailed to a group. Each individual could research and answer them, then submit their answers (is they chose to) for further discussion online with the group.

1 Thessalonians 1 Study Questions

1. Who wrote this letter? To whom it is written?

2. Where is Thessalonica and how is Paul associated with it? (See Acts 17)

3. What does Paul think of these believers?

4. What does he know about them and what is he encouraged by?

5. What is Paul's attitude towards their relationship with God? (v. 4)

6. What surrounded Paul's preaching of the gospel in Thessalonian church?

7. How had the Thessalonians responded to the word?

8. In verse 7 Paul points out something very important about the Thessalonians, what is it?

What does that Greek word (*tupos*) mean?

9. Can verse 8 be said about our church or even you in particular? Why or why not? What do you think about this Thessalonian church based upon this description?

10. What separates our God from idols? Do we preach that? How?

11. What is the current state of the Thessalonians? Is this a passive or active state?

12. What does Jesus do for the believer? What is the literal meaning of the word deliver (*rhoumai*)?

1 Thessalonians 2 Study Questions

1. Why does Paul remind the readers of the details surrounding his visit?

2. What would it be like to preach amid much opposition? How do you think it would affect

you?

3. From verse 3, what 3 defenses does Paul give of his ministry among them?

4. What is Paul's motivation for preaching the gospel? What does it mean to be a man-pleaser, as opposed to a God-pleaser?

5. Was it Paul's goal to be well-liked and highly thought of?

6. What does the illustration of the nursing mother teach us about Paul?

7. How did Paul feel about the Thessalonians? How was that expressed?

8. Why might Paul have written verses 9-10?

9. What three techniques did Paul use? Why? Who are they?

10. What was significant about Paul's message that the Thessalonians recognized?

11. What does the Word of God do in the lives of believers?

12. Paul and the Thessalonians have persecution in common. Why were they hostile to Paul and the Gospel?

13. What does Paul say about those who attempt to restrict the preaching of the Gospel?

14. Who does Paul think is the leader of this movement?

15. What do the Thessalonians mean to Paul?

1 Thessalonians 3 Study Questions

1. Why might Paul give such a sound reference for Timothy?

2. What two goals would Timothy have in Thessalonica? Why?

3. What do you think is happening when troubles come your way? What does Paul say about such things?

4. Who does Paul again accuse of trying to spoil the fruits of the message?

5. What was Paul afraid the Thessalonians would think of him and the perhaps the Gospel message?

6. What was the report?

7. What is the reward for the missionary and the evangelist and the pastor?

8. Does there need to be more preaching beyond the Gospel message?

9. What term does Paul use to describe God?

10. Why does he seem to want to see the Thessalonians so badly?

11. What was his wish for them? How does this happen?

12. What does verse 13 refer to?

13. Who are the "holy ones" of verse 13?

1 Thessalonians 4 Study Questions

1. What was one thing Paul did talk about when he was with the Thessalonians?

2. What does he want from them? Why?

3. Where does Paul's authority come from?

4. What is God's will for the Christian? Why?

5. Are verses 3-6 just off the top of Paul's head or is he responding to something?

6. Christians are called to live what kind of life? Why?

7. What is the contrast in verses 9-10 to that which has proceeded them? What do you think is at the root of this whole discussion?

8. What is the encouragement in verse 10? And the plan for a good Christian life in verse 11-12? What do you make of that plan?

9. Ambition (to be found of honor). Is this followed or not in society today?

10. What was something Paul had not had time to get into while he was with them?

11. Who are those who are asleep? Who are those who have no hope?

12. What is implicit in the "if" (compare NIV to NASB) clause of verse 14? How certain can we be of the return of Christ?

13. List the series of events given here by Paul. Compare them to Revelation 19:11-21.

14. Who are the "dead in Christ?"

15. Why is this event often referred to as the "Rapture?"

16. What does Paul imply by his use of the word "we" in verse 17? Why does Paul write about these events?

1 Thessalonians 5 Study Questions

1. What was the issue at the end of chapter 4 that Paul had not instructed the Thessalonians about?

2. Why does Paul not need to write to them about the end times?

3. How is the "Day of the Lord" different from those events described in chapter 4?

4. Who will be saying "peace and safety?" Who will experience destruction (note: not annihilation)?

5. Who won't escape this time?

6. What is different about believers? Why won't they be taken by surprise?

7. What encouragement does Paul remind them of in verse 5?

8. How does the "sleep" differ from that in chapter 4? What should be the status of the Christian?

9. What did God not destine Christians for?

10. What does that refer to (remember the context)?

11. What does it mean to be awake or asleep?

12. What assurance does Paul give Christians?

13. What should be the outcome of these words?

14. What approach does Paul use at the beginning of his final instructions in verse 12?

15. What does Paul want the "brothers" to do?

16. What is that nature of this "respect?"

17. Who is he talking about? What are their responsibilities?

18. Why should they be held in highest regard? What does this mean?

19. By implication then, what is their responsibility in living at peace?

20. List the 9 other things that Paul expects of Christians within the church? (vv. 14-18)

21. What does it really mean to give thanks in all circumstance? How does this apply to your life right now? Are you doing it or not?

22. Why might they have looked upon prophecies with contempt? What is prophecy in the church age?

23. How are we to examine prophecy?

24. Who sanctifies?

25. What three aspects of our life represented in verse 23?

26. What can we be certain God will do for us? Why? How does this relate to what Paul said Romans 8:30?

ABOUT THE AUTHOR

Evan D. Baltz's passion for the Word of God is evident in his writings. Over the last 25 years his presentation of the Word, whether it be through proclamation, teaching, or the written word, has dynamically drawn people into a deeper understanding of God. He combines an irreverent sense of humor with a scholarly reverence for Scripture, making his books enjoyable, thought-provoking, and instructive for young and old, new believer and theologian.

Evan graduated from Bethel Theological Seminary with a Master of Divinity degree in 1992 after receiving his Bachelor's degree in Psychology from Iowa State University. He has served both as a youth pastor and senior pastor, as well as speaking at numerous conferences and retreats. Several of his articles and sermons have been published nationally.

Made in the
USA
Monee, IL